MEDIEVAL LIVES

Nun

ROBERT HULL

W
FRANKLIN WATTS
LONDON•SYDNEY

First published in 2008 by Franklin Watts

Franklin Watts
338 Euston Road
London NW1 3BH

Franklin Watts Australia
Level 17/207 Kent Street
Sydney, NSW 2000

A CIP catalogue record for this book is available
from the British Library.

Dewey number: 940.1

ISBN 978 0 7496 7736 7

Printed in China

Franklin Watts is a division of Hachette Children's
Books, an Hachette Livre UK company.

Artwork: Gillian Clements
Editor: Sarah Ridley
Editor in chief: John C. Miles
Designer: Simon Borrough
Art director: Jonathan Hair
Picture research: Diana Morris

Picture credits:
AKG Images: 29. Austrian Museum of Applied Arts Vienna/Bridgeman Art Library: 25. Bargello Museum Florence/Alfredo Dagli Orti/The Art Archive: 23. Bibliotheque Municipale Poitiers/Gianni Dagli Orti/The Art Archive: 27. Bibliotheque Nationale Paris/AKG Images: 37. Bibliotheque Nationale Paris/Giraudon/Bridgeman Art Library: 39. British Library London: 15, 19. British Library London/The Art Archive : front cover, 21. British Library London/Bridgeman Art Library: 33. British Museum London/Bridgeman Art Library: 34. Chateau de Versailles/Giraudon/Bridgeman Art Library: 24. Fitzwilliam Museum Cambridge/Bridgeman Art Library: 35. Erich Lessing AKG Images : 11. Musée de l'Assistance Publique, Hopitaux de Paris/Archives Charmet/Bridgeman Art Library: 14. Musée Condé Chantilly/Bridgeman Art Library: 10, 13t. Musée de l'Hospice de Villeneuve-les-Avignon/Gianni Dagli Orti/The Art Archive: 22. Musée Lambinet/Archives Charmet/Bridgeman Art Library: 20. Musée Muncipale St Germain-en-Laye/AKG Images: 30. Musée des Tapisseries Angers/Lauros Giraudon/Bridgeman Art Library: 38. Museo Nazionale de Lazzo di Venezia, Rome/AKG Images: 18. Museo Provincial de Bellas Artes Zaragoza/Bridgeman Art Library: 41. Gerhard Ruf/AKG Images: 9. Topfoto: 13c. Victoria & Albert Museum London/Bridgeman Art Library: 26. Victoria & Albert Museum London/Eileen Tweedy/The Art Archive: 7, 31. von Linden/AKG Images: 17.
Every attempt has been made to clear copyright. Should there be any inadvertent omission please apply to the publisher for rectification.

CONTENTS

INTRODUCTION

The medieval period of European history, from about 1000 to 1500, was full of momentous events. In 1066 England was conquered by the Norman French king, William the Conqueror and his nobles; France and England fought a long gruesome Hundred Years War; Christian crusaders battled Muslim Arab armies; and in 1348, the Black Death killed around a third of the population.

Feudal society

At the beginning of this period, European society was 'feudal'. Kings owned the land, granting it to warrior knights, or barons, in return for war-service. Knights rented 'tenements' to those below them, holders of manorial estates, including religious houses, and they in turn rented land in return for money or services to those below them, down to the peasants. But from the 13th century onwards, the growth of towns, trade and travel, and money transactions, started to dissolve this 'feudal' structure.

Monastic life

Almost everyone in medieval Europe believed in a Christian God and followed the teachings of the Roman Catholic Church, headed by the Pope in Rome, Italy. Religion was at the centre of their everyday lives. Some people chose to take this further and joined religious communities. There were several different types, or orders, each following their own religious rules, including: Benedictine, Cistercian, Carthusian, Cluniac, Franciscan and Dominican. There were monasteries for men and convents, – or nunneries – for women.

Religious communities

Although, throughout the medieval period, many more men than women, lived monastic lives, a powerful religious revival in the

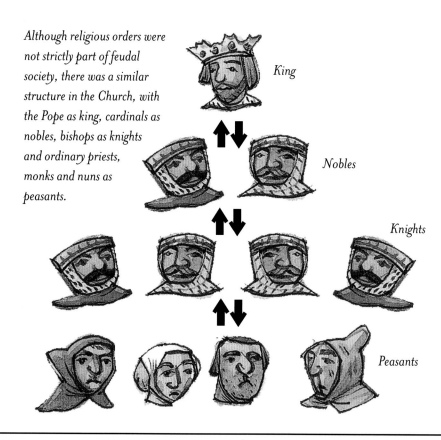

Although religious orders were not strictly part of feudal society, there was a similar structure in the Church, with the Pope as king, cardinals as nobles, bishops as knights and ordinary priests, monks and nuns as peasants.

King

Nobles

Knights

Peasants

12th and 13th centuries brought many women into religious communities. There were only 13 nunneries in England in 1066. During the next 150 years, 120 more were founded.

Many women entered nunneries in devoted dedication; others, because marriage was, economically, not an option. Around 1066 most women seemed to marry. However, as the dowry, the wedding 'gift' provided by the father of the bride, became more expensive, and the population rose, parents with several daughters found the price of marrying each to a man of adequate status beyond their reach. An alternative career, as a nun, could be had for a smaller 'entry' payment. It cost less to marry the Son of God than a mortal man, one wit said.

Vows

Nuns took vows of poverty, chastity and obedience, and some also promised to remain within the enclosed community. Enclosure meant remaining in the physical confines of the convent, and ensuring that any visitors belonged to the officially sanctioned few.

Chastity meant remaining always in the state of virginity. Obedience involved unquestioning adherence to the instruction of superiors. Poverty meant no private possessions, and for some groups no communal possessions except what were necessary for survival – a garden to grow food in. These ideals were hard to live up to. It was stressful to live communally, sleeping in dormitories and eating in refectories. This book will follow the story of a merchant's daughter who decides to become a nun in the 14th century.

This medieval Italian fresco depicts St Clare (1194-1253), a nun and friend of St Francis of Assisi. She founded an order of nuns, the Poor Clares. She is shown in her nun's habit.

BIRTH

T he woman is expecting another baby. The father has asked a monk for assistance with a safe birth. He has brought two precious relics: pieces of the sail that belonged to St Peter's fishing boat on Galilee. The relics will stay with the mother until she is safely delivered.

The only people in the large bedroom that is to be the birth chamber are the midwife and women of the household. The mother-to-be came to the room a month ago, with her women, after taking communion, and saying farewell to her husband, for the time being at least. The room has been specially hung with rich cloth, and carpeted. Candles burn and some windows are covered.

Prayer and preparation

The household prays – the monk prays. For the baby, the prayer is that it will survive long enough to be baptised. For the mother, that she will be safe and survive to be purified in church after 40 days.

Medieval women believed in magical aids to a safe birth. Striking a bell three times at certain moments helped. Semi-precious stones were useful, especially aetites or eaglestones, which eagles took to their nests to help breeding. Scrolls with promises written on them could be laid across the mother's belly. It also helped to obtain from churches the religious relics they hired out: the Virgin Mary's girdle, another Virgin Mary's girdle, a link from St Peter's chains, a finger bone belonging to St Stephen, and so on, all of which helped to ensure safe delivery of the baby.

Although this religious picture depicts the birth of John the Baptist, the scene in a wealthy medieval house would have been much the same, with the mother recovering from the birth in bed and the baby about to be washed.

The medieval baby girl would have been baptised in a stone font like this one dating from about 1150 in Skjeberg church, Norway.

There is rejoicing and relief in the large house that evening for a baby girl has been born, another daughter, not a male heir. There are entertainments the same night; a minstrel and music, dancing, food and drink.

The father is a prosperous merchant who can afford to summon a monk with relics, and supply all the entertainment. What's more, his other daughters have not yet taken expensive dowries off into marriages.

Baptism

The baptism takes place as soon as possible – after two or three days – since an unbaptised child is in danger of going to a place where God is not; that is, to Hell, according to the Church. The mother is at home, unpurified after the uncleanness of giving birth, unable for 40 days to touch anything holy or enter a church.

In the church porch the priest makes signs of the cross on the baby's forehead and asks her in Latin – speaking to the godparents – first, whether she renounces Satan, and second, what it is she wants. To be baptised, the godparents say, speaking on behalf of the baby. They enter the church and go to the font. There, the priest, holding the baby, makes more signs of the cross, sprinkles her with holy water from the font, names her and hands her back to the godparents.

Churching

After 40 days comes the mother's 'churching', the service of purification, which she attends joyfully, wearing a new dress. After her churching there is more entertainment. The servants share in the excitement and happiness but also hope that the celebrations aren't premature, remembering all the babies they know who died.

CHILDHOOD AND EDUCATION

The baby is nursed and cared for by the women of the household. She grows stronger quickly. The mother herself is soon busy again managing the large household. She sees her new daughter every day, but the baby's daily breast-feeding, washing, dressing, putting-to-bed and everyday care are the responsibility of the nurse and the women of the household.

The wise lady

The 14th-century French writer, Catherine de Pisan, says that the wise lady should:

❖ *... watch over her children and their upbringing diligently, even the sons... although ... it is the father's responsibility to seek a teacher... The wise lady who loves her children dearly will be diligent about their education. She will ensure that first of all they learn to serve God, and to read and write, and ensure that the teacher makes them learn their prayers as well. The wise lady will try to get the children's father to agree that they be introduced to Latin and that they understand something of the sciences.* ❖

Early years

Servant-women play with the baby, rock her in the cradle and sing to her, and give her lots of the kissing and hugging babies need. They watch when she begins to crawl to make sure she stays safe.

The baby becomes the toddler, the toddler the young girl. As she grows older, and unlike boys in other families, she does not go exploring around the town on her own. She goes out with the servants sometimes (above), and with all the family to church.

Reading and writing

By the time she is five, she is learning to read and write at home, like her sisters. Her father has found a respectable woman to teach her, who is knowledgeable and quiet; her conversation is pleasing, and she can speak Latin.

Her parents begin to consider the idea that she might continue her learning in the nunnery outside the town. For a modest fee, the nuns accept a few children as pupils. One or two even board in the nunnery. With this in mind, the teacher is asked to instruct her in religious matters. Now she can read, she has books of devotion, including a Psalter, and books about conduct and behaviour.

pires · ⁊ conueme pur uim
tement ⁊ pur urance te qui
est meismement necessaire.

 amons nos
te/mais par
Quar es au
nos ne parla
la maniere r
nere. Et si n
aucun por te
maniere req
tost apres t
tenenre del
re que nes l
faire ⁌Iu c
greement r

ja consele. vi lui te de Redon q̃ a
rede ldouas q̃ est la sin qume p
ac de laic.   ⁌ xxiii

os auons es
uit en ce liure

This manuscript illustration shows a medieval school lesson in progress.

Nunnery dress was plain, even sombre, not what young girls were used to. They evidently dressed cheerfully. This description comes from K. Bartsch's *Altfranzosische Romanzen und Pastourellen (Old French Romances)*:
❖ *She had a little shirt of linen, a white pellice of ermine, – stoats' fur cloak – and a bliaut – dress – of silk. Her stockings were embroidered with gladioli designs, and her shoes, by which she was tightly shod, had May flowers.* ❖

The convent school

Her mother takes the decision, when the girl is seven, to send her to the convent 'school'. She will not board there, not now at least. A servant will take her each day.

She goes to the school. She likes the nuns and the calm atmosphere of the place. There is even a schoolmaster there, teaching Latin; his pupils have to speak Latin, nothing but Latin, in the schoolroom and also in the street! She learns some simple Latin and she learns to sing. She is taught with other girls and boys from the town, as well as the nunnery's postulants – girls who wish to become a nun. At times, they are

Medieval children learned their letters from a wooden hornbook, which had its written text covered with transparent animal horn to protect it.

joined by professed (committed) nuns who do not understand Latin well enough to sing the services confidently; they even make mistakes reading from their slates.

TO THE NUNNERY – POSTULANT

After three or four years at the school, in a room in the outside wall of the convent, the young girl thinks she would like to be a nun. As a first step, she must proclaim her desire to be one, and become a 'postulant', then later a 'novice'. She is only 11; to be a novice she must be older – 13 or so.

Her parents are pleased for her to become a nun. It means one less marriage dowry to find. She will be cared for in the nunnery, and safe, and have companions in religion, and if she wants to take her final, binding vows when the time comes, she can. If not, she can leave.

If she stays, she will vow to aspire to many things, but three things especially. In humility she will obey instructions; she will remain always a virgin and praise chastity; she will give up thought of personal possessions. She will be silent most of the time; talk with visitors, or conversation with other nuns, is allowed in the 'locutarium', but silence is expected at most other times. Mealtimes are silent. Nuns listen to readings, using sign language to say 'pass the bread please'.

Sisters at an island nunnery welcome a novice (left) and receive a sick person into their infirmary (right). From a 15th-century manuscript illustration.

The dowry

In the meantime, her father has to pay her entry fee – which is voluntary in theory, but not in practice, though smaller than a marriage dowry. As it happens, he also has to provide some furniture, including a bed, and a habit – a set of nun's clothes.

At home she wore colourful, pretty clothes, made from expensive materials like silk. No longer. Her habit is a white tunic and scapular – a piece of cloth with an opening for the head – a leather belt, a black mantle and veil. The design is simple and the wool coarse, unfinished and not dyed. She has to wear the full habit when she's asleep too.

The other three young postulants are from nearby. Their fathers are merchants or farmers with large houses, but not mansions.

Others in the nunnery

It surprises her that not all the nunnery's inhabitants are nuns. There are two or three older women who are not professed, as well as two widows, one with a daughter living with her as a postulant. And three girls between the ages of six and nine board in the nunnery. Their families pay well for their keep and board, so the prioress accepts them, though the bishop will probably demand that they leave when he visits.

There are women from poorer families too, not nuns, who have taken vows, but are 'lay sisters', the nunnery's working women.

There are some girls who are unhappy there. After a year they will be given the opportunity to say whether they want to take the nun's vows or not. They will leave.

The abbess (chief nun) cuts the hair of a postulant, from a 14th-century manuscript.

The future nun will take time to get used to not seeing her family, and to the convent's stern rule of silence.

She becomes familiar more quickly with areas of the convent she did not visit as a pupil: the churchyard and cross-shaped, stone church inside the high wall, the bellhouse by the church, the prioress's rooms next to it, and the cloister where, in the centre of it all, she can walk and meditate.

Convent buildings

By the church is the chapterhouse, where the nuns discuss the affairs of the convent - one of the few times the nuns are allowed to talk. On another side of the cloister are the refectory where everyone eats and adjacent kitchens, and the sleeping quarters, the 'dorter'. Close to the dorter are the latrines or the lavatorium, placed over the stream that flows through.

She discovers the hall, then across the space of the great court, the infirmary with its own chapel, the lodging house for visitors, and the locutarium or 'parlour', where nuns can receive certain visitors, usually family members; and where at certain times conversation is permitted on religious subjects and in the presence of senior nuns.

Medieval facts

Some nunneries had small separate quarters for permanent paying guests, like the widows of those who gave generously to the nunnery. These paying guests were called 'corrodians'. They attended church, seeing the elevation of the host at Mass, but could not sit in the nuns' choir. Viewing galleries were sometimes built at one end of the church for them or any other 'seculars' present.

In their spare time, the nuns walk and read in the convent's cloister (covered walk).

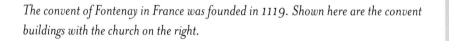

The convent of Fontenay in France was founded in 1119. Shown here are the convent buildings with the church on the right.

Farm buildings

Her mother had described those places, but the schoolroom was well away from the outbuildings and sheds, and she was not prepared for the noise of the pigs and lambs and dogs, which she can hear even from inside the church. She had expected calm and quiet, not the ring of metal from a smithy, or carpenters' hammers, or horse-drawn carts rumbling in and out through the gatehouse; or cooking and baking and brewing smells like those at home.

She watches lay sisters seeing to the animals, washing and mending, cleaning shoes, and the rest. She catches glimpses of the priests going to and from their rooms over the gatehouse and in chambers in the outer court.

She peers into the stables, the kiln, the milkhouse and the granary. She finds her way to the garden and the orchard, and the small court for the nuns only.

She thinks how all this building huddles inside walls that no nun ventures beyond without special permission. She wonders whether, if she does become a nun, she will step outside them ever again. For now at least, she is free to come and go with the lay sisters working in the fields, like the other boarding children.

Chapter of faults

The chapterhouse was for non-spiritual meetings of the whole nunnery. The 'chapter of faults', for example, was a regular meeting of the whole convent where nuns admitted faults and were asked by the prioress whether they wished to accuse others. The prioress decided on punishments. Salome Sticken, a 15th-century prioress at the convent at Diepenveen, in the Netherlands, inflicted various humiliations on offenders:

❖ *She castigated those sisters by making them wear humble clothing, and torn and patched surplices and veils. She instructed someone to wear an apron on her head, or use buttons from old nightshirts as a paternoster [rosary]… She would give them tasks like begging for bread at other tables in the refectory, or kissing the feet of sisters or asking forgiveness or submitting to being beaten.* ❖

TAKING THE VEIL – NOVICE

At 13, after two years of living freely amongst the nuns, the young postulant decides she would like to enter the community, and 'take the veil' as a 'novice'. The whole convent gathers in the chapterhouse to see her before the prioress, and hears the prioress ask her: 'What is your request?'

She has been well prepared: 'I wish for the mercy of God and to join the community of nuns.'

After more questions and answers, the prioress takes her hands in her own. 'On behalf of God and ourselves, we receive you here and grant you fellowship with us.'

'Amen,' says everyone; and they fuss decorously round her.

Two Holy Nuns *by the Master of San Jacopo – an Italian painting of 1399.*

Investiture as a novice

There is a ceremony of investiture in the chapel, at the altar. The new novice receives her habit, not the habit of the professed nun, but a white veil and sleeveless scapular – a long choir tunic. To remind her that her past is rejected, she is asked to tread on the fur-lined cloak she brought with her to the convent.

The novice learns about being a nun. She is placed in the care of a 'mistress of novices'. Her guidance will be partly moral, to do with how the novices should behave and comport themselves obediently and humbly towards their seniors. She will also learn how to chant the eight daily services in Latin, how to sing loudly and softly, and any other skills that nuns need, such as embroidery.

Medieval facts

In the 12th century at least, there was probably no uniform habit for nuns. A ruling of St Benedict had stressed the importance of plain clothing, but did not mention colour. A decree of 1235 from the General Chapter of the Church stipulated cloak or cowl, and black veil. But dress generally must have been sober, even dowdy. Nuns used only undyed cheap cloth of black, brown, white or grey. Some nuns were known as 'white nuns', others – even of the same Cistercian order – as 'black nuns'.

The programme of religious training for the novice of 14th century Windesheim Convent in the Netherlands was part social, part moral, part spiritual:

❖ *And Katharina taught Griete how she should humble herself before her sisters... and how she should go to them in silence and subjugation and be attentive to them, and how she should burden her heart with daily contemplation of the suffering of our Lord...* ❖

Profession as a nun

When she is 15, the novice is offered a choice: to leave the convent or, by composing a letter, to profess formally her desire still to be a nun. She writes her letter, vowing to be obedient, embrace poverty and remain a chaste virgin. The novices who can't write have their letters written for them, which they sign with a cross.

In the ceremony of profession in the chapel, the novice lies prostrate before the altar, her new habit waiting beside her. It is consecrated with holy water. She removes her old habit, and puts on the new one. She is veiled again, this time in black. Standing by the altar, she reads her letter aloud, kisses it, and kneels again on the altar steps. Mass is sung.

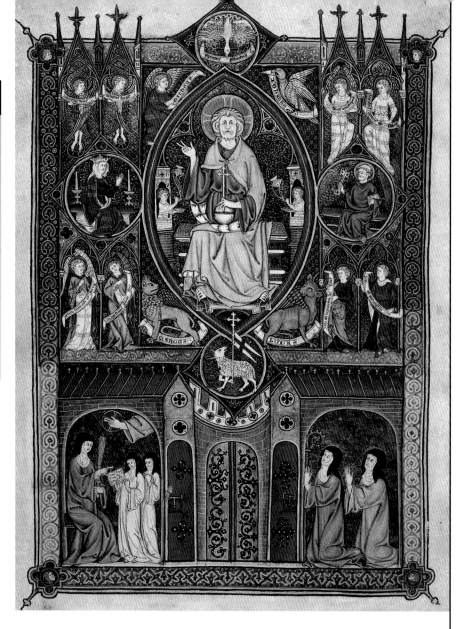

God and the saints look down on nuns in this 13th-century manuscript painting. The picture at the bottom left depicts a nun in charge of two novices. She holds a birch rod to administer discipline.

In her 15th-century *Chronicle and Necrology of Corpus Domini*, Sister Riccoboni of Venice tells the story of Lucia Tiepolo, known for her preoccupation with virginity, who took:

❖ *that* [Benedictine] *habit at the age of 11 and lived in it for more than 80 years... From the moment she was enclosed she never wanted to see a man's face. When doctors or teachers came, she fled; sometimes she could not escape quickly enough on account of her age, so she covered her face with a scapular. The young women asked her: "Why do you flee like that?" She replied: "My dear daughters, even now I fear for my virginity."* ❖

DAILY LIFE –
THE OFFICES

The new nun is fervent in prayer, the praise of God and spiritual exercises. Her days celebrate abstinence from normal pleasures, and commitment to her vows of poverty, chastity and obedience. For her, the fullest expression of devout spirituality is the daily reciting or singing of the eight daily services – or 'offices'.

The nuns' choir

At each office she enters the church with the others, bows in front of the altar, and takes her place in the nuns' choir. The nuns are 'dead to the world', and perform their liturgical tasks – singing, chanting and praying – out of sight of the world, in the nuns' choir. Their choir, in the chancel, is raised like a gallery, physically separate from the canons below them performing the sacraments, and from other worshippers in the nave.

The new nun is aware that there, beyond the screen that hides them, are the lay sisters, and further back from them, the permanent residents, the corrodians, with the rest of the lay people, convent guests, villagers, estate-workers and so on. Of course, these lay worshippers are more likely to be present during daylight hours than when the nuns begin or end their long day of worship.

Within her community, the abbess was all-powerful. This is the 13th-century crozier of the abbesses of a Cistercian convent in France. Normally only bishops carried this symbol of authority.

Medieval facts

The nuns aspired to sing or recite the offices well, without making mistakes that might offend God, and please the Devil. Most of them knew little Latin, and sang by memory, making it all more of a risk. In a story called *The Myroure of Oure Ladye*, written to amuse some 15th century nuns, a 'little devil' called Titivillus goes round collecting all the nuns' singing mistakes; he picks up all the hundreds of dropped syllables he finds lying around, all the mispronounced and left-out words from their singing and chanting and puts them in a bag to take to 'his master', the Devil.

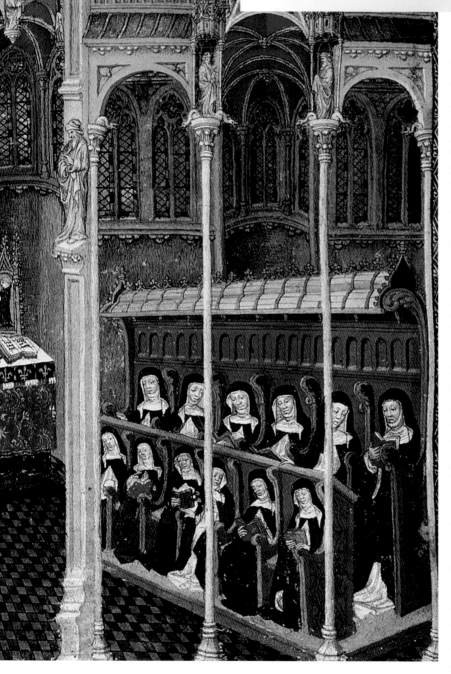

'Rules' for nuns set out everything about how they should behave as enclosed nuns worshipping communally. There are even instructions in one Nuns' Rule for avoiding rude behaviour after lauds:

❖ *None shall push up against another wilfully, nor spit on the stairs as they come up or down — unless they tread it out forthwith.* ❖

The offices

The first office, matins, is at midnight in summer, an hour later in winter. It is sung together with lauds. As summer dawn breaks, the nuns go to bed for two or three hours, till the office of prime at about 5 am.

The weekly 'chapter of faults' comes next, on the appropriate day; there are prayers, then the prioress details faults in the nuns' religious observances, and asks them to confess their own and inform the chapter of other nuns' faults. The new nun dare not say anything about others, and waits in trepidation for her own conduct to be faulted. But she is newly professed, and no-one speaks badly of her.

Through the day come the other offices — tierce at about 7 am, sext at about 9 am, mass at 10 am, then nones about 2 pm, community mass or vespers in the late afternoon, and finally compline, at around 6 to 7 pm in winter, an hour or so later in summer.

Nuns singing in the choir of their church, from an early 15th-century manuscript.

THE INNER LIFE

The nun feels intensely the meaning of what she sings and says during the religious services. The hours in the choir are the most significant of her day. But she aspires in other ways too, to total adherence to her vows, and the renunciation of worldly pleasure. The pleasures of food and speech, for instance, are suspiciously worldly, and the temptation to enjoy them is best fended off by extreme abstinence.

The coronation of the Blessed Virgin; *a painting of 1453 by Enguerrand Quarton. Images like this assisted nuns with their prayers.*

Exercises

Most sisters devise personal exercises to help them in their devotions. They do these exercises because they wish the mind to be flooded with the divine every moment of the day, giving the Devil no opportunity to sneak in.

One sister prostrates herself before Christ as soon as she wakes. Another has a routine of so many exercises — repeating texts learnt by heart, intensely contemplating one moment in Christ's life — that others tell the time by her movements and speech.

Abstinence

Abstinence frees the soul for God. The nun has renounced the world for the cloister, and marriage with a man to live as the bride of Jesus Christ. She is overjoyed to be near Him, when the eucharist brings her 'the body and blood of Christ'. For some, abstinence is difficult, and they punish themselves. They fast, pray ceaselessly without sleeping, even beat each other with whips.

Clare of Assisi, who founded the Second Franciscan Order, or order of Poor Clares, often fasted severely, taking no food on three days every week, and little on the others.

Sister Riccoboni, in the chronicle of the Venetian convent of Corpus Domini, 1395-1436, mentions certain sisters as worthy of special praise for their devotions:

❖ *These women practised great abstinence. Many dragged their mattresses away and slept upon bare planks... They frequented the choir so much they could hardly wait to go to the office. Some of them told me that when they entered the choir they seemed to see an angel who led them in singing. When one sister was in ecstasy, she saw white puffs like cotton issue from the mouths of the sisters as they sang. She also saw the Devil waiting eagerly to see if anyone left out a syllable, to make a note of it.* ❖

One or two sisters practise humility by 'stealing' work – often the worst work, such as slaughtering animals or cleaning the lavatorium. They sneak in beforehand so that the work is already done when the duty nuns arrive.

Reading

Apart from the offices, the most important spiritual activity for the young nun is silently reading devotional books, and copying extracts. She also enjoys the reading aloud which one nun performs for the others.

Private meditation, prayer and reading – for those who are literate – are fitted in between communal attendance at the offices. About an hour-and-a-half is set aside for reading, before vespers, and after the evening meal. Nuns who wish to read more, as the young nun does, in their free time, on Sundays or on feast days, need the prioress's permission.

The young nun knows she must take care that reading does not become a pleasure of a worldly kind.

Other aids to devotion could be three-dimensional. This ivory sculpture of the Virgin and Child dates from the end of the 13th century.

DAILY ROUTINE

T he nun finishes her breakfast of bread and ale in silence, at about 5.30 am. After a morning tidying and cleaning her cubicle in the dorter, performing private prayer and meditation, and attending the offices, there is dinner.

Mealtime

She and a few others sometimes eat as a 'family', in the cellaress's room. It is a relief to escape the difficult nuns, like the ex-prioress who shows her 'humility' by grabbing the least tasty bits of food before anyone else starts eating.

The nun's two meals a day are cooked and served by lay sisters. There is meat sometimes, and always on feast days – of which there are more than a hundred! Her drink is nunnery-brewed ale, and wine sometimes. Bread and water is the only fare on Fridays and other fast days, though novices eat proper food.

This picture of nuns dining is much later than our period (c.1710) but the scene probably didn't change that much. A sister reads aloud (left) as the others eat in silence.

A chasuble (garment for a priest) worked by nuns in the 13th century.

Work

In the afternoon every nun is engaged in useful work. The young nun teaches postulants to read and write, and girls and boys from nearby. There are also children whose fathers have gone on crusade, leaving wives and children in the nunnery. This practice worries the bishop, as all boarding does; girls and small boys have even slept in the dorter, despite letters forbidding this.

Other nuns spin or weave, or embroider vestments – religious garments. One or two are engaged in copying religious texts. There is also work to do in the convent garden, and in the orchard. But apart from nuns on official nunnery business, no-one goes to work outside the walls. The work needed in the fields – haymaking, tending animals and so on – is done by the lay sisters.

Silence and signs

There is a short supper after compline. Were it not for being silent they could talk over the doings of the day, but sign-language is permitted. A nun flapping her hands loosely is saying, 'Please pass the fish.' 'Wine, please,' is moving the forefinger up and down the thumb.

Nuns on nunnery business out in the world sometimes see something worth retelling. But juicy news like:

Medieval facts

In some nunneries much routine physical work – cooking, dish-washing, washing clothes, emptying chamber-pots, brewing, baking, churning, wool-combing, tending animals – was done by 'lay sisters'. These women were not professed nuns, but they took monastic vows, and lived in the community. They wore habits slightly different from the nuns', and followed divine services in the main body of the church not the chancel, where the choir-nuns were. Lay sisters' work allowed choir-nuns to spend more time on prayer and spiritual exercises, though as some nuns realised, this put at risk the balance between physical work and prayer that St Benedict, the founder of perhaps the best-known monastic order, the Benedictines, believed was essential to nuns' spiritual lives and general well-being.

'I saw the cellaress riding behind the chaplain on his horse this afternoon,' is difficult to relate, even using all the 106 signs in the book.

After dinner it is straight to bed, supposedly, in the dorter, though some nuns meet to talk. Sleepless nuns must not get out of bed.

ENCLOSURE

The enclosed nature of convents might be compromised in various ways. Popes often granted permission for great personages to visit. Thomas of Gloucester had permission to visit monasteries of enclosed monks or nuns six times a year, with 20 persons of either sex. Not surprisingly, nunneries protested. In 1375, the Pope ordered the local bishop to agree to the petition of the prioress and nuns of North Berwick 'for perpetual enclosure… they being much molested by the neighbourhood and visits of secular nobles and other secular persons.' And Oxford students often made a nuisance of themselves hanging round local nunneries.

The nun has become 'dead to the world'. She is cut off from it emotionally, so she is not free, for instance, to give or receive the kind of love that she knew with her family. She hardly ever sees any of her family now. A nun's love is exclusively for God.

She is also cut off from the world physically. Her convent is enclosed, separated, as far as it can be, from the world outside. She hears of some nunneries' attempts at complete enclosure, when the sisters tried to support themselves entirely from working their own land. They usually struggled and, in extreme cases, began to starve, and had to be helped.

A 15th-century tapestry depicting the search for spiritual truth. The two nuns in the middle are enclosed within their convent.

Total enclosure

So 'total' enclosure, if it means not holding land and property as well as the nuns staying strictly inside the convent walls and not even going out to collect alms, means nunneries can't support themselves. They cannot be both 'contemplative' – so doing little or no work beyond observing a spiritual rule – and totally 'enclosed' – and so cut off, physically, from the world round them. If their work does not feed them, and if they have no contact with people outside, how can they survive?

But even when nunneries possess land and an income, 'enclosure' can be extreme in other ways, and feel total. One convent she hears of has only one external door, placed high in the nunnery wall and reachable only by ladder. Foodstuffs and other goods are brought in on a horizontal wheel, called a 'rota', like a revolving tray.

Attempts were made throughout the medieval period to compel nuns to stay in their convents. In 1298 Pope Boniface VIII decreed, in a document called 'Periculoso' for short, that all nuns, including prioresses, were to remain perpetually enclosed in their nunneries, unless gravely ill, and receive no visitors, except by special licence:

❖ *... so that being altogether withdrawn from public and mundane sights, and all opportunity for wantonness removed, they may more diligently preserve for Him in all holiness their souls and bodies.* ❖

When the Bishop of Lincoln came visiting Markyate to put this into effect the nuns chased him off, throwing the document at his head.

Saint Radegund retreats from the world into her nunnery, from an 11th-century French manuscript.

Farms and fields

This nunnery, though, has farms and fields to support it, tolls and tithes, rents and fines. It was founded with money from a bequest, and since then has acquired more farms and land. It functions as a manor functions, with tenants holding land which nunnery officials manage, while the nunnery itself stays enclosed, focused on the spiritual life.

Even then there is the question of how the nunnery should relate to the men it relies on and employs, and to those in the outside world with whom it has economic ties. Should a steward or shepherd or carpenter live within the bounds of the convent? Which sisters, if any, should meet the reeve, or any other man?

Enclosure was often physically absolute. The Corpus Domini convent in Venice had one door. That door had three locks; each of the three keys was held by a different nun.

CELLARESS AND LIBRARIAN

After several years in the nunnery, the nun takes up the office which the prioress wishes her to have, that of cellaress. In this medium-size convent of about 40 nuns, the cellaress is one of the 'obedientiaries', officials with particular responsibilities.

Here, the other obedientiaries are: a sub-prioress to assist the prioress; a treasuress who collects rents and fees and pays bills; a chantrist to look after the music and the running of church services; a sacrist who has charge of all the church fabric and candles and plate and altar cloths and so on; an almoness in charge of charity; a chambress in charge of clothes; and a kitcheness in the kitchen.

The cellaress's role

The cellaress looks after the food and drink of the convent, laying in stores from the market (right) and the nunnery's farms, and organising its bakery and brewery. She arranges meals, and engages cooks and servers. The nun is proud to serve God in those ways.

The prioress is pleased, because her cellaress is a dedicated nun, who will not abuse her freedom when she goes outside the nunnery to the market place, the farms or the shops in town. She will be level-headed, not silly or frivolous, when she meets the men she must speak to outside the nunnery walls.

A library

The cellaress is also keen to buy books for the nunnery, and look after them, so she takes up this secondary responsibility. In modest-sized nunneries, roles are often doubled up, and though there is no official librarian, it helps to have someone responsible for books, and parchment, and writing utensils.

The nun realises that, though aspects of true spirituality are

There might be limitations imposed on what nuns could read or write. In 1455 the prioress of Windesheim in the Netherlands was banished by the General Chapter, apparently for encouraging 'mystical' literature. The resolution displacing her says:

❖ *No nun or sister, no matter what her status, may... copy books which contain philosophical teaching or revelations... on penalty of imprisonment... It is the responsibility of all to ensure that they are burned as soon as they are found.* ❖ Books relating mystical experiences – revelations – had been the most characteristic religious women's literature.

Nunneries had libraries, but seldom much money to buy books. In 1372 William Wokkyng was found guilty of ambushing, with seven accomplices, a certain rector, and with robbing him of three horses, two girdles harnessed with silver, and books worth £10. One of the books, worth about £3, was later sold to the nunnery at Dartford. Evidently they were interested in the kind of books that secular clergymen read.

A well-educated nun writing at a desk, from a 15th-century woodcut.

neglected in this nunnery, the life of the spirit flourishes strongly in others, and especially in the reading of spiritual works copied and translated from Latin into the vernacular. Most nuns cannot read Latin, but are willing to try master-works of the spirit such as *The Revelations of St Bridget* in their own language.

One or two nuns who are deeply engaged in this study also copy manuscripts for others to read; the cellaress herself is translating an ancient literary work, *Distichia Catonis*, into English verse from the Latin.

The world outside enters the nunnery in various ways, because the nunnery is part of the world. Local people make bequests to the convent; a croft or pasture is left to the priory, in return for the singing of a weekly Mass. The nunnery's church is also the parish church; the convent uses one side, the parish the other.

The nunnery needs villagers to work as its officials – steward, bailiff, reeve and others. It needs peasants to plough and sow and reap, and tend its animals. The cellaress meets them all.

Visitors from the outside world

The convent receives visitors. The bishop calls. The cellaress meets traders, as do other obedientiaries involved with buying goods for the nunnery. They need all sorts, from candles and fabric to building materials. Merchants call to inspect fleeces from the convent's flock.

A nun (middle) watches a conjuror perform a magic trick in this painting by Hieronymus Bosch (c.1450-1516).

Nunneries' economic ties to a locality were often exactly those of the manor's, and records of them were kept in the same way. The list of tenants and services drawn up at Chatteris Abbey in Cambridgeshire in the early 14th century includes holders of one acre who paid a rent of '12d and a hen', villeins holding 18 acres and a cottage who had to perform 52 jobs annually, including roofing, mowing, ploughing, and other things, as well as owing 'boon-works', and 'one hen and 16 eggs annually', and a rent of 2s 6d. The abbess demanded high entry-fines, too, for taking over the rent of land: 60s for 18 acres and a messuage in 1312.

Family members visit sometimes, for a brief hour, and talk in the locutarium, providing a companion is present. The cellaress's sisters flaunt their latest clothes and jewels. Perhaps once a year, the family are allowed to have dinner with her, bringing her news of the world. She has little news herself, except the sad tale of a woman living in the nunnery who has heard of the death of her husband on crusade.

Nuns in the world

The tide of affairs flows out, taking obedientiaries into the world, on nunnery business. The prioress and sub-prioress ride off to see lawyers and auditors, usually appointed from nuns' families. The prioress is called to see the bishop, or invited to gatherings in the town, which she says she attends in the interests of the nunnery. Useful bequests and endowments might follow such contacts.

And of course the local women engaged as lay sisters are out and about daily, in the fields and on the roads. They come and go frequently.

Out in the world – a prioress on her horse, from a manuscript of Geoffrey Chaucer's Canterbury Tales.

Nuns are also permitted, perhaps once a year, to visit their families, even friends, especially when they are ill. This is a new fashion, and not one that the bishop encourages. Nuns should never go on travels, amongst secular people, staying in common lodging-houses, hearing scrurrilous tales and bawdy songs on the road. But where discipline is relaxed, of course these things happen.

PRIESTS AND NUNS

Nuns have left the world of men, and the company of men, but they are closely surrounded by it. Men drive the carts that clatter in and out through the gatehouse all day long. Ploughmen, shepherds, haywards, foresters and ditchers; these men run the farms whose produce and rents enable the nuns to live for God.

The priest's spiritual assistance

Men are needed for the nun's spiritual work. Nuns cannot hear the confessions of other nuns, or receive the eucharist from them. Only male priests are permitted to administer those sacraments. Confession to the priest (right) is made without eye-contact with him, through a grille.

Life without men

A French song advises against the nun's life:

❖ *Get married, girls, find a nice young man; don't go there, girls, to rot behind a grille, inside their walls.* ❖

A 14th-century Latin song from Germany has the nun say:

❖ *All night long I'm kept awake; how glad I'd be to embrace a young man.* ❖

Dancing nun

According to a 14th-century visitation record, one nun:

❖ *... did pass the night with Austin friars at Northampton and did dance and play the lute with them till midnight and on the night following passed the night with Friars Preacher at Northampton, luting and dancing in like manner.* ❖

The priests are also valuable spiritual advisors. At certain times in the week, one of them speaks to the nuns on particular subjects. The young cellaress finds this advice helpful, and makes notes of what is said.

Latin

The priests read documents sent in Latin to the prioress. The prioress knows some Latin, but not enough: much less than her cellaress. Priests occasionally perform menial tasks, too, like washing down the altar. The priests live, dine and sleep in their own quarters, apart from the nuns, but still inside the walls of the nunnery, in the gatehouse rooms, and in chambers in the outer court.

There is also the bishop. The prioress is mistress of the nunnery, and has power there, but its control and direction is ultimately in his hands. He sends the prioress regular letters reminding her that the nuns should not wear jewellery, or be seen in the town, or own pet dogs, or take a favourite hawk into church.

On the other hand, sometimes he has had to restrain them from excesses of devotion that might damage their health.

Danger

For the nun, though, men are also a danger, and a threat to her vows. She goes amongst the world of men more than any other nun, but she avoids all unnecessary speech and eye-contact, and chance encounters. She knows how easily lapses occur, and rumours circulate.

Shocking things are indeed seen occasionally, and at times the worst of stories will circulate, told in shocked whispers, of nuns who have run off with minstrels, or nuns who have become pregnant by priests.

Naughty chaplain

Chaplains occasionally displeased the nuns they served. Sir Henry, chaplain of Gracedieu in 1440-41, goes out haymaking with a cellaress, and in the evening she rides back behind him on his horse. Not only that, he:

❖ *... busies himself with unseemly tasks, cleansing the stables, and going to the altar without washing, so staining his vestments.* ❖

Naughty neighbours: in this manuscript picture, a monk and a lady are put in the stocks (a punishment device that pinned the legs) for being too familiar with each other.

POVERTY AND PERSONAL POSSESSIONS

A rich 13th-century brooch. Nuns couldn't own such fine items.

The nun gave up all her personal property when she became a nun. She gave it to the nunnery, to be held in common. Clothing, rings, jewels, pets, food and allowances of money were all things she was forbidden to have in her possession. Gifts from her family are permitted, but are held by the prioress, all together, as communal property.

At the beginning of her time in the nunnery, not even her habit was her own. When the one she was wearing needed washing, she took another, newly cleaned, from the common pile.

Poultry problems

Allowing personal property in a nunnery created difficulties: even hens could be a problem. Visiting St Aubin in Normandy, in 1265, a bishop noted that:

❖ *Because several of the nuns keep cocks and hens and often quarrel over them, we ordered that all cocks and hens were to be fed alike and kept in common and the eggs distributed equally amongst the nuns and that hens should sometimes be given to the sick to eat in the infirmary.* ❖

Two years later he notes that nothing has been done 'about the poultry'.

Aspiring to the ideal

The ideal was always hard to live up to. It is hard to manage with nothing you can call your own. It has now been agreed that there is no point leaving family gifts and bequests – money, rings, chalices, candlesticks, manuscripts – hidden in dark boxes, and that individual nuns can keep them. Now they have these things, some nuns even want keys for their boxes.

So there is now private property in the nunnery. There is also money for all nuns to spend. It has been agreed that each nun should have a small annual allowance for clothes. Those with only this allowance can supplement it by knitting and embroidering things that they can sell – silk purses for instance – to women from the village, or each other.

Money

With their 'clothing' allowances, some nuns – against the rules – buy food from women who come to the windows, or slip into town on the excuse of seeing a sick friend or relative, and run up debts at shops. And now that some nuns sometimes eat their own food in 'families', separate from those in the refectory, it seems that private money and property may not help communal living.

Devout nun though the cellaress is, clothes and jewellery are not things she will ever totally lose her desire for, or ever succeed in resisting trying to get hold of.

The cellaress sees that the idea of property is changing. But even she hardly notices that, like all the nuns, she feeds 'her' hens and collects 'her' eggs from them. She does realise though how easily quarrels start over eggs laid in the 'wrong' nest.

A page of female saints from an early 16th-century prayerbook – the sort of lavish item that a nun from a wealthy family might have been allowed to keep.

A VISITATION

The bishop makes an official visitation once a year to find out if the rules of the order are being observed and to determine if the nunnery is in 'good health', spiritually and financially. He speaks with the nuns and asks them one by one all kinds of questions about life in the nunnery.

Lapses

The bishop is told who has gone out without permission, who has missed a service. He finds out who talks, who sleeps late, who dawdles near the priest and who has ridden on horseback with the reeve.

Such offences are common. This year there are more worrying problems. The cellaress has described how nuns can now make small purchases of clothing and other things, and now they want keys for their boxes. One or two have been observed wearing rings.

The local bishop often visited convents to make sure rules were being followed.

In the infirmary, sick nuns could be better cared for. They seem to have no more food than the others, though money has been set aside to buy it; they have even been criticised in their absence at the chapter of faults.

Silence

It seems the fundamental rule of silence is not observed in the church, or the cloisters, or the refectory, or the dorter. There is surreptitious chatter going on behind every pillar, it seems.

The most serious offence is that divine service is performed inadequately. There is giggling and talking during offices; nuns doze off or leave early with an excuse. Snoring has been heard. And frequently, the bishop

finds, the services are hurried through, mispronounced and gabbled, some nuns having not troubled to discover the meaning of the Latin they sing and speak. There has also been gossiping and drinking after compline.

An unpopular prioress

The bishop discovers that the prioress is no longer popular. She has guests to dinner, when she dresses up, curls her hair, and wears furs and jewellery. She goes out riding too.

She lets the sub-prioress meet the nuns in the chapterhouse to take advice about the business of the convent, then makes decisions on her own on important matters that concern everyone, like which merchants shall handle the convent's crop of fleeces.

She has let things slide, nuns say. Woods have been sold to make money, but the church roof lets rain through on their heads. Their clothes have holes in. They hold up their gloved hands to show him.

Often, convents were visited by royalty, as this manuscript illustration shows.

The bishop hears all the complaints, and writes down that the nunnery is undergoing a crisis. He also knows from the treasuress that no important bequests have been made recently.

DIFFICULT TIMES

The plague of a few years ago took several nuns from them. Many workers in the fields died, too. Since then, the cellaress feels, nothing has been the same. She wonders what the future holds. The nunnery still owns all its farms, mills, markets and manor court, but like other manors, it is falling on hard times. In particular, the bequests of land and property from local people have almost dried up.

Famines and plagues were viewed by medieval people as manifestations of God's anger against the sinful.

Food

Not even the nunnery food, which she is responsible for, is as good as it was. At times when harvests have failed, only bread, cheese and ale have appeared on the table. The nuns have had to provide some food themselves, donated by friends or family. They wonder aloud whether the prioress is still eating well in her rooms, and whether the canons' daily fare is as meagre as their own.

The bad harvests may be partly to blame, but other aspects of the nunnery's economy are faltering. The fleeces are not fetching the prices they did. Rent revenue is falling, and they come in more slowly. Work drags out. Ditching, fencing and building repairs are not done promptly.

Clothing

The nunnery's difficulties affect the nuns directly, and personally. Clothing is a particular problem. They have had only one pair of shoes a year recently, a tunic every three years or so, and the last change of cloak was six years ago. And when their clothes get tattered nowadays, they are not replaced.

It is often cold and damp in the nunnery, too. In the winter months older nuns feel the cold badly. It is not surprising that some nuns have started to receive legacies of clothing from their parents – usually the young ones.

The cellaress and the more concerned nuns discuss all kinds of explanations. The prioress cannot manage her household properly. The alterations done in the last few years have been too costly and ambitious. Some farmers get away with not paying their rents. Bequests have stopped.

A stern sister in her seventies says that it is God's will that the nuns should be punished, for failing to live according to their vows.

War was an ever-present threat to the peace and stability of the community. An army sacks a town in this 15th-century painting.

DEATH

The cellaress is still in her forties, but she has been made ill by constant worry about how to keep the nunnery supplied with food and drink; and her constitution has been undermined by cold and damp, and by too much riding out in the world.

The prioress suggested that it should be a younger cellaress who went riding here and there in all kinds of weather but she chose to carry on. And because she was as devout as ever, she allowed herself no respite from the convent's gruelling daily round of offices.

Her life of prayer and work over, a nun dies in the convent's infirmary.

Last illness

Her health worsened. She allowed herself to miss matins and lauds for a few days, but not to enter the infirmary. Now, not surprisingly, she has fallen seriously ill, and has difficulty breathing.

She feels she may be near death. A vision she had, of being taken up to heaven, has convinced her, and also reassured her. She reflects that she is only forty-something, but thinks of the young ones, in their early twenties and teens even, whom she has watched die in the nunnery.

She has asked that the nuns sing hymns. They also recite the Lord's Prayer round her, over and over.

She wishes to receive the last rites and Extreme Unction to set her on her eternal path, to be given the viaticum, of the bread that is the body of Christ. Only male priests can administer this. The sacristan rings a bell to summon a canon. He comes with three other canons as witnesses, and a lay brother.

Final gathering

At the sound of a clapper, all the nuns come. The entire body of the convent is gathered round the dying nun's bed. The prioress asks a nun to describe a good quality of the dying sister, something to remember her by; the nun describes how once the dying sister remained motionless, not moving a limb, rapt in spirit, for a whole day and a night.

The prioress asks another nun, who recalls her love of poverty and recounts how she heard her say once that she would 'rather have a devil in her cell than a shilling'.

After listening to this recital of her virtues, the nuns wait for her last words, hoping to hear something significant or memorable. They are rewarded by hearing her say, before she dies, 'Obedience is the shortest path to eternal life.'

Christ welcomes the faithful into Heaven in this 14th-century Spanish painting.

GLOSSARY

Abbess/abbot ❖ the head of a nunnery or monastery

Artisan ❖ a craftsman or woman, such as an embroiderer or blacksmith

Bequest ❖ a legacy – a gift detailed in a will

Bishop ❖ from the Greek *episcopos*, meaning 'overseer', the highest rank of churchman in the diocese, a division of church terrain and control

Boon-days ❖ extra days of work on demand, on the lord's or lady's land

Canon ❖ clergy attached to a college church or cathedral; 'secular' canons lived in their own houses; 'regular' canons observed a Rule

Cellaress ❖ a nunnery official responsible for food supplies and trade with the world outside

Chancel ❖ the main space at the east end of a church, with the altar, separated by a screen from the nave

Chapterhouse ❖ a meeting space for the whole convent

Choir ❖ part of a church, in the chancel, where the nuns worship

Clerk ❖ a churchman, a literate man, or someone looking after accounts

Cloister ❖ covered but open area round a courtyard or green space

Confession ❖ the private admission of sins to a priest

Convent ❖ a gathering together of women living communally

Corrody ❖ a grant of lodging, food and drink, usually made in return for a generous gift

Diocese ❖ an area of churches and religious communities and lay people under the control of a bishop

Divine offices ❖ religious services, usually seven or eight a day, sung and recited at certain hours

Due ❖ an amount to be paid

Dowry ❖ the money and goods a father gave his daughter when she married

Feudalism ❖ the system of holding land in return for agreed services or works or money

Fine ❖ a fee or charge

Endowment ❖ a gift of money, usually to a religious or educational foundation

Eucharist ❖ the sacrament of the Lord's Supper

General Chapter ❖ an annual meeting of the heads of religious houses

Grammar ❖ codified rules of a language

Hayward (or heyward) ❖ village official responsible for arranging the hay crop

Herbal ❖ a book of medicinal herbs, with diagrams

Host ❖ the bread that is 'the body of Christ' in the holy communion

Investiture ❖ the act of formally putting someone into office

Laity ❖ from the Greek *laos*, people, the unordained (ie not in religious orders) people of the church

Liturgy ❖ formal prayers and rituals

Manor ❖ a feudal estate tenanted by a lord, usually inherited, with its own manor court

Mark ❖ a coin worth 13s 4d

Mass ❖ the central religious service of the medieval church, enacting the ceremonial consumption of bread and wine, 'the body and blood of Christ'; sung by the priest in Latin

Money ❖ 1d = 1p, 240d = 100p, 20s (shillings) = £1, 1 mark = 13s 4d [= 65p]

Monastery ❖ a place where nuns, monks, or both, live religiously, away from society

Nave ❖ the main part of a church

Necrology ❖ a convent's 'book of the dead' with brief accounts of each nun's last days

Novice ❖ no longer a postulant but not yet a nun

Order ❖ religious communities belonged to one of a number of 'orders' founded by different spiritual leaders, whose 'rules' differed slightly

Payment in kind ❖ payment with articles of produce, eg eggs

Pittances ❖ extra food given to everyone on holy days

Postulant ❖ a woman who expresses her desire to become a nun to an abbess

Priest ❖ the clerk in charge of the church; sometimes a rector or vicar (meaning substitute for rector)

Primer ❖ a small handwritten manuscript with extracts for children to learn to read from

Prioress ❖ in Benedictine convents, the second in command after the abbess; and the head of a religious house without the legal status of an abbey

Profession ❖ when a novice 'professes', undertaking to live according to the vows of an order, she becomes a nun

Psalter ❖ the Book of Psalms

Regular clergy ❖ those living according to a 'Rule', and usually in an enclosed community

Relic ❖ an object venerated by believers because of its associations

Rule ❖ a founder's or reformer's statement of basic values and practices for living in a particular order, usually enclosed but not always

Screen ❖ (or rood-screen) a division, usually of wood, between chancel and nave

Secular ❖ not separated from the world; 'secular' clergy live in society

Tithe ❖ the annual payment due to the church or lord of one-tenth of a villein's produce

Toll ❖ the right to make strangers bringing goods to town pay an amount [a 'toll'] on what they brought

Vestment ❖ religious garment, like a cloak or robe

Villein ❖ a peasant tied to the land, who farmed strips of a village's 'common field'

Vows ❖ formal promises to God

TIMELINE

910	Abbey of Cluny founded
c.1000	Scandinavia and Hungary converted to Christianity
1066	William of Normandy crowned King of England
1066	13 nunneries in England
c.1080	writing of very influential *Speculum Virginum* (*Mirror for Virgins*) for reading by nuns
1088	papacy split - two competing popes
1096	first crusade begins
1098	Cistercian order founded
c.1100 on	powerful religious revival in the 12th and 13th centuries bringing many women into religious communities.
1146	St Bernard of Clairvaux preaches (announces) second crusade
1162	in England, Thomas Becket consecrated as Archbishop of Canterbury – quarrels with King Henry over church's power
1163	cathedral of Notre Dame begun in Paris
1170	murder of Becket by knights believing it to be what Henry wanted
1174	Henry does penance for murder of Becket
1177	foundation at Amesbury (perhaps part of Henry's penance) of nunnery with membership of French nuns
1189	third crusade begins – fails to capture Jerusalem
1207	order of St Francis formed
1208	King John of England quarrels with Pope - Pope bans church services in England
1208	crusade against Albigensian heretics in France
1214	barons demand charter of liberties from John
1215	Magna Carta
1216	St Dominic's order of Friars – travelling preachers - approved by Pope
1217	fifth crusade
1230	English King Henry III campaigning in France
1235	black veil stipulated for nuns
1248	seventh crusade
1260	Chartres cathedral consecrated
1305	Clement V becomes Pope – moves papacy to Avignon
1348–1349	arrival of Black Death in Europe
c.1350 on	decline of nunnery membership after plague – down to 30 per cent of pre-plague figure in England
1361	plague breaks out again
1377	Avignon 'captivity' of papacy ended
1389	first translation of Bible into English
1395–1436	Sister Riccoboni compiling *Chronicle and Necrology of Corpus Domini*, Venice
c.1400	Christine de Pisan writing *Treasure of the City of Ladies* and other spiritual works
c.1400	beginning of 'Modern Devotion' movement in Netherlands
c.1400 on	increasing ignorance of Latin and French amongst nuns – in England bishop's instructions sent out in English
1414–18	end of Great Papal Schism
1450	invention of printing with moveable type
1490	Edward IV's youngest daughter enters nunnery
1530s	dissolution of monasteries and nunneries in England

INDEX

These are the lists of contents for each title in *Medieval Lives*: